Lulu Mayo

HOW TO DRAW A
MERMAID
AND OTHER CUTE CREATURES

WITH SIMPLE SHAPES
IN 5 STEPS

Andrews McMeel
PUBLISHING®

FROM LULU

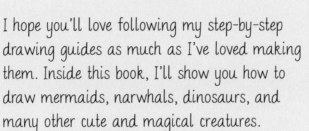

I hope you'll love following my step-by-step drawing guides as much as I've loved making them. Inside this book, I'll show you how to draw mermaids, narwhals, dinosaurs, and many other cute and magical creatures.

Each character is brought to life using simple, recognizable shapes that anyone can draw. Don't worry if you make a mistake. Your drawing doesn't have to be exactly the same as the example. Let your imagination run wild and create your own new creatures!

LULU MAYO

THE STEPS

The clear, step-by-step instructions for each creature in this book are easy to follow.

Outlining the body and head gives you a great starting point. Use a pencil to create your initial drawing.

Add simple shapes to start bringing your character to life.

1.

2.

3.

4.

Add all of the elements. Then erase the pencil lines you don't need.

Go over the outline in pen if you'd like.

5.

Finally, add color.

NOW PICK UP YOUR PENCIL AND DRAW!

NARWHAL

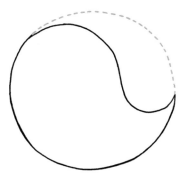

1. pencil in a circle, then add
a dip to make it a teardrop

2. two little leaf shapes
make the tail

3. add eyes, mouth, and
two triangles for flippers

4. long tusk, plus a wavy
line for the tummy

5. give it a
blue hue

Draw your narwhal here.

Turn this page into a happy underwater home full of narwhals. Use the shapes to get you started.

NESSIE

1. connect a big and little oval with two lines

2. a triangle makes the tail

3. four small triangles become the flippers

4. add a top hat, bow tie, cane, and a dot for the eye

5. give it a jazzy look

Your Nessie's next.

4

Practice your Nessies here. What colorful
patterns and fancy headwear might they have?

How does
he do it?

MANATEE

1. circle head and oval body

2. heart-shaped flipper and tail

3. dots for the eye and nose

4. add a bow

5. a colorful outfit

Draw your own.

Doodle more marvelous manatees floating around in the sunshine.

Come on in, the water's lovely.

FAIRY

1. raindrop head, wavy dress, and sausage arms

2. another wavy line for the hat and dots for eyes and mouth

3. triangles for legs and leaf-shaped wings with your own funky pattern

4. add a magic wand

5. make her colorful

Now you try.

Create your own magical fairies with epic hats.

Draw me
some friends,
pleeeease.

JELLYFISH

1. wobbly rectangle

2. dots for eyes and mouth

3. sausagey shapes
for tentacles

4. add dotted lines

5. add some color (this
one's a strawberry jelly)

It's your turn.

Add more wibbly-wobbly members to the jelly band.

Join the jelly jam!

MERMAID

1. draw a horn with a circle at one end and two leaf shapes at the other

2. add two crescents around her waist, plus arms and hands

3. dots for the eyes and mouth, and flowy hair

4. wavy lines for scales and two hearts for her bikini top

5. add lots of color

Try it out.

Create lots more mermaids (and mermen) with funky hairdos.

Shake,

rattle,

and roll.

HAMMERHEAD SHARK

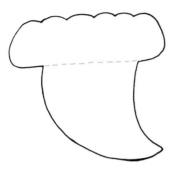

1. horn shape with a
fluffy rectangle on top

2. dots for eyes and a
curvy line for the smile

3. little triangles
make the fins

4. leaf shapes for the tail and
two triangles for a bow tie

5. add some color and he's
ready for a night on the town

Now you have a go.

Doodle more hammerhead friends below.
Don't worry—they're very friendly.

AVOCADO BOY

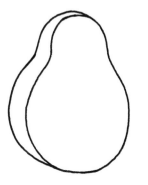

1. pear-shaped body with a repeat wave on one side

2. dots and a semicircle make the face

3. rounded triangles for arms and legs

4. add stalk, round tummy, and a cross for his belly button

5. color him in and it's time to hit the gym

Av-a go at your own.

Doodle a whole avocado family here. Don't
forget to include a little baby avocado.

Sleepy avocado

Hula-Hoop avocado

Old avocado

STARFISH

1. draw a star

2. dots for eyes
and a happy mouth

3. bow tie

4. lines make your
starfish shine

5. give it some color

Draw yours here.

Draw starfish of all different shapes and colors.

Pop starfish

Rock starfish

DRAGON

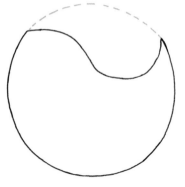

1. circle with a dip

2. dots for eyes and mouth, circle for head, and lines for tummy

3. triangle legs and arms

4. little wings and semicircle spines

5. don't forget the color

Your turn!

Flying dragons, water dragons, fire-breathing dragons.
What dragons would you like to draw?

21

TURTLE

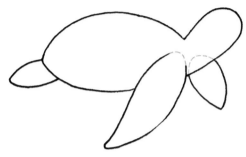

1. two ovals

2. leaf shapes for legs

3. big eyes and smile

4. add shell lines and a hat

5. make it colorful

Now you try.

Different shell shapes make different turtles. Experiment!

Sea turtle

Shy turtle

Tortoise

23

PANDA CUPCAKE

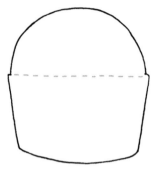

1. semicircle on a rounded rectangle

2. wavy line and vertical stripes for the cup

3. oval eyes and a little T for the nose

4. two round ears

5. color and decorate

Now try your own.

Fill the shelves with more awesome animal cupcakes.
How about including some koala or puppy cakes?

CLOWN FISH

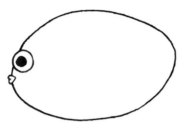

1. start with an eye
and a heart mouth, then
add an oval body

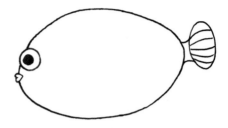

2. oval tail connected to
the body with lines

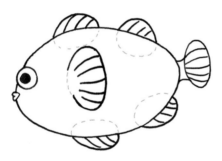

3. more ovals for fins

4. add a hat and
stripy pattern

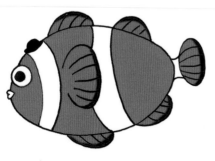

5. make it orangey and bright

Have a go.

Create your own undersea scene.

Have you seen my hat?

GNOME

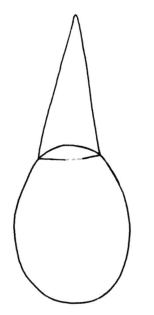

1. oval and triangle

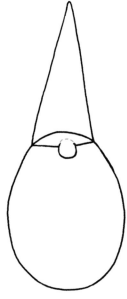

2. circle for the nose

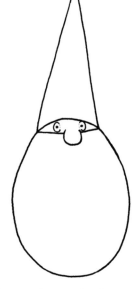

3. ovals with dots in the middle for eyes

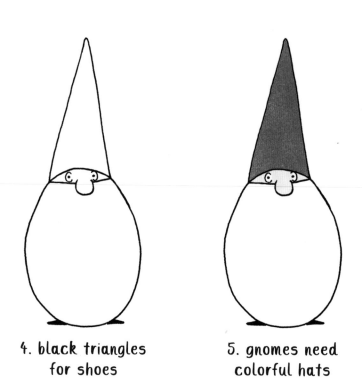

4. black triangles for shoes

5. gnomes need colorful hats

Give it a try.

Gnomes all have their own personalties. Fill this
page with as many different gnomes as you can.

Aaah...
CHOOO!

Sneezy gnome   Sleepy gnome   Grouchy gnome   Cheery gnome

SEASHELL

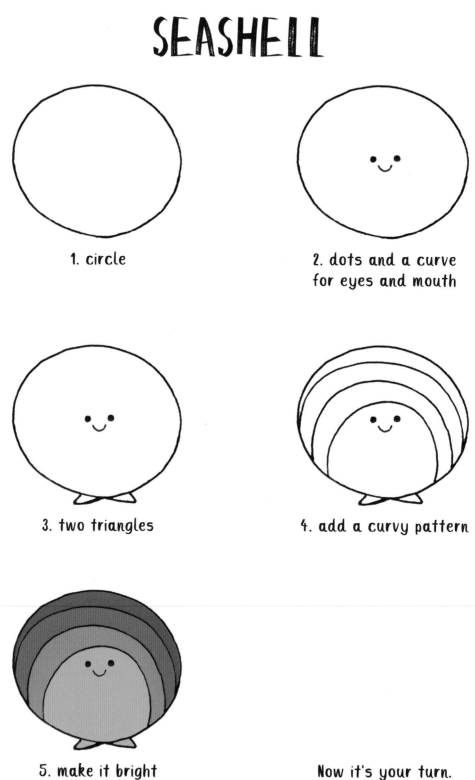

1. circle

2. dots and a curve for eyes and mouth

3. two triangles

4. add a curvy pattern

5. make it bright and colorful

Now it's your turn.

Use these shapes as inspiration to
create your own adorable seashells.

Pick me!

PURRMAID

1. oval with a dip
at the bottom

2. triangles for ears and leaf
shapes for the tail

3. draw a face and use
triangles for paws

4. add a bow tie and scales

5. pick some
paw-some colors

Draw yours.

FROG PRINCE

1. draw a circle with four triangles sticking out

2. big eyes and smile

3. circle for his tummy, with a bow tie on top

4. add crown, flowers, hands, feet, and a belly button

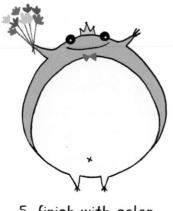

5. finish with color fit for a prince

Draw your own fabulous frog.

Draw more froggy royalty.

DOUGHNUT LION

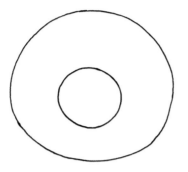

1. two circles make
the doughnut

2. circle ears, dot eyes,
heart nose, and a big
W for the snout

3. long sausages for
the front legs and a
heart-shaped back leg

4. a hat, bow tie, and tail

5. finish with color
and sprinkles

Try it!

Create doughnut lions of different yummy flavors.

SEAHORSE

1. circle head, oval body, and swirly tail

2. long snout and big eye

3. heart-shaped wings and wavy hair

4. tummy lines and a bow tie

5. add your own colors

It's your turn.

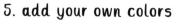

Create your own seahorses. They can
be as magical and colorful as you like.

You're so magical!

I know.

RACCOONICORN

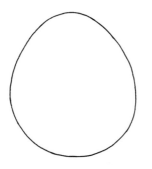

1. draw an egg

2. heart-shaped face

3. horn, curly hair, and triangle arms and legs

4. tummy, belly button, and a bow tie

5. rainbow colors

Have a try.

Use these shapes to start some
magical mash-ups of your own.

Pandacorn

Bunnycorn

Kittycorn

DOLPHIN

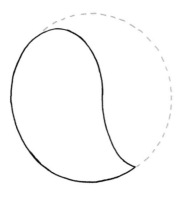

1. turn a circle into an upside-down teardrop

2. triangles for flippers and leaves for a tail

3. a line with a dot in the middle makes the mouth, then add eyes and a nose

4. curvy line makes the tummy and triangles make the bow tie

5. a splash of color

You're up!

Try using different shapes and colors
to create your own happy dolphins.

Spinner
dolphin

Spotted dolphin

Irrawaddy
dolphin

CATCUS

1. circle on top of two
rounded rectangles

2. eyes, whiskers, and nose

3. triangles for ears and
feet and a sausage tail

4. add flower, spines,
and dotted lines

5. color it up

Your turn.

Fill these shelves with cute cacti and catci.

T. REX

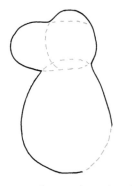

1. three ovals make the body

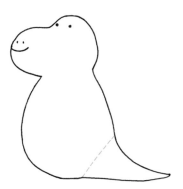

2. eyes, nose, mouth,
and triangle tail

3. triangles for arms
and legs, plus tiny claws

4. add a bow tie,
hat, and tummy

5. a pop of color
and he's ready to go

Your rex next.

Fill the field with dino-pals.

NINJA SLOTH

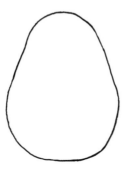

1. egg shape

2. sausages for arms
and triangles for legs

3. oval face, with eyes and nose

4. add a sword and belt

5. color it in

Sketch your stealthy
sloth here.

Use the shape to draw a secret spy
sloth hanging from the tree branch.

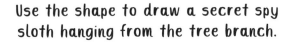

Mommy ninja sloth

Halloween's
not here yet.

Mummy sloth

SEA LION

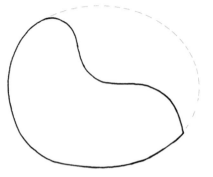

1. oval with a dip at the top

2. triangles for the front flippers, hearts for the tail

3. dots for eyes, heart, and stick for nose

4. add a hat and bow tie

5. finish with flair

Now draw yours.

Experiment with different shapes to
create your very own sea lion family.

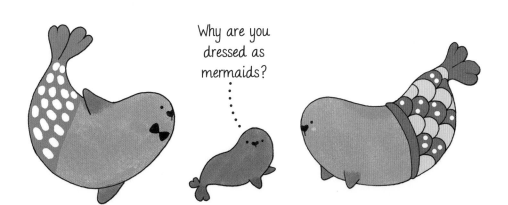

Why are you
dressed as
mermaids?

MERMICORN

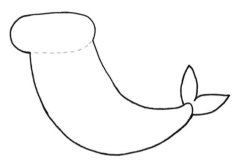

1. horn with an oval at the top and two leaves at the bottom

2. oval ear, fluffy clouds for hair, and striped cone for the horn

3. oval arm and dots for eyes and a nose

4. wavy scales

5. add color

Go for it!

Fill the sea with musical mermicorns.

PUP CUPID

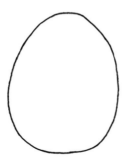

1. oval body

2. oval ears, triangle
legs, and cute face

3. fluffy wings
and triangle paws

4. add bow and arrow,
plus a tongue and tail

5. add plenty of color

Create your perfect pup.

Fill the sky with more cupids spreading puppy love.

Elephant pup

SUSHI

1. fluffy oval and
rounded rectangle

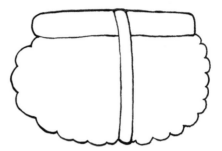

2. tall, curved rectangle

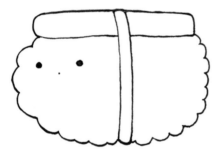

3. add dots for eyes and a mouth

4. rounded triangle hands

5. finish with color

Give it a go.

What's on the menu? Create your own cute sushi set.

ORCA

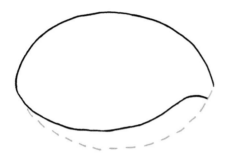

1. oval with a dip
at the bottom

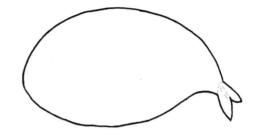

2. leaf shapes for a tail

3. triangle fin and flipper

4. add eye and patterns

5. complete with color

Now you try.

Use these shapes to try out different poses.

Whale hello there.

ROBOT

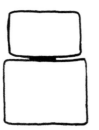

1. two boxes, joined in the middle

2. rectangle arms and arcs for hands

3. rectangles with semicircles on the bottom make the legs

4. add antennae and big eyes

5. dress your robot up

Try it out.

Draw a whole troop of robot friends. Try out different shapes and patterns to make each one unique.

Bleep bleep.

How to Draw a Mermaid and Other Cute Creatures

Andrews McMeel Publishing
a division of Andrews McMeel Universal
1130 Walnut Street, Kansas City, Missouri 64106
www.andrewsmcmeel.com

First published in Great Britain in 2020
by Michael O'Mara Books, Ltd.
9 Lion Yard, Tremadoc Road, London SW4 7NQ

20 21 22 23 24 RLP 10 9 8 7 6 5 4 3 2 1

ISBN: 978-1-5248-5381-5
Library of Congress Control Number:
2019953411

Made by:
Shenzhen Reliance Printing Co., Ltd
Address and location of manufacturer:
25 Longshan Industrial Zone, Nanling,
Longgang District, Shenzhen, China, 518114
1st printing—1/13/20

W www.lulumayo.com   f @lulumayoart   @ @lulu_mayo_art

Writers: Lulu Mayo and Gary Panton
Cover design: John Bigwood
Designer: Jack Clucas
Editor: Jean Z. Lucas
Art Director: Diane Marsh
Production Manager: Tamara Haus
Production Editor: Amy Strassner